"Hope springs eternal in the human breast:
Man never is, but always to be blest."

*~ Alexander Pope*

## Also from Kathy Ashby

Carol 'A Woman's Way' *(DreamCatcher Publishing) 2009*

# From the Rim of the Bowl

by Kathy Ashby

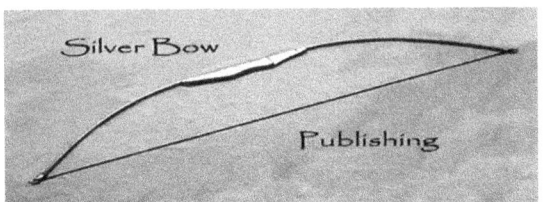

720 Sixth Street, Unit #5
New Westminster, BC V3L 3C5
CANADA

Title: From the Rim of the Bowl
Author: Kathy Ashby
Publisher: Silver Bow Publishing
Cover Art: "Twilight Aurora Borealis" painting by Candice James
Layout/Design: Candice James
Edited by: Allan Briesmaster

All rights reserved including the right to reproduce or translate this book or any portions thereof, in any form without the permission of the publisher. Except for the use of short passages for review purposes, no part of this book may be reproduced, in part or in whole, or transmitted in any form or by any means, either by means electronically or mechanically, including photocopying, recording, or any information or storage retrieval system without prior permission in writing from the publisher or a licence from the Canadian Copyright Collective Agency (Access Copyright).

www.silverbowpublishing.com
info@silverbowpublishing.com
ISBN: 978-1-77403-279-4  paperback
ISBN: 978-1-77403-280-0  e- book
© Silver Bow Publishing 2023

Library and Archives Canada Cataloguing in Publication

Title: From the rim of the bowl / by Kathy Ashby.
Names: Ashby, Kathy, 1953- author.
Description: Poems.
Identifiers: Canadiana (print) 20230551149 | Canadiana (ebook) 20230551157 | ISBN 9781774032794
    (softcover) | ISBN 9781774032800 (Kindle)
Subjects: LCGFT: Poetry.
Classification: LCC PS8601.S428 F76 2023 | DDC C811/.6—dc23

*From the Rim of the Bowl*

This poetry collection is for Gaia,
ancient Greece Goddess of the Earth

and

I thank my husband, Brian,
for his perfect and total support
during the writing of this poetry collection.

*From the Rim of the Bowl*

## Contents

**EARTH**

Amen to the Park in the North / 13
Dust / 14
Ode to the Raspberry / 15
The Raymond Valley / 16
Ready – Set – Day / 18
Someday in Late Autumn / 19
Eat the Day / 21
What the Meek Shall Inherit / 22

**YOUNG WOMEN**

Infamous Eve / 25
Puddle bridge / 26
Gimme Lights / 28
Nana – Look and See / 29
Child - Look and See / 30
You may become aware / 31
It Stands Still for Her / 32
Roommates / 33
Guilt on the Menu / 34
Gotta Have It Once a Month / 35

**SNOW**

Winter Menu / 39
Snow Glitterati / 40
Made You Look / 41
White Silence / 42
Big Dollop for the Town Tailor / 43
Joy of the Snowfall / 44
Poof / 46
We See Music / 47
In October's Cool Climate / 49

## LOVE AND OTHER THINGS

Sarajevo / 53
I Know Nothing About Tides / 54
HEY / 56
Tune of Words / 57
Bright Morning Thoughts / 58
Love Gamble / 59
Spaces / 60
Listen to You / 61
Mistress / 62
You are in love / 63
Beautiful Black / 64

## ELDERS

Benefit of Within / 67
Slow Cooker / 69
You Know That You're Not Really Important / 70
Eyes Bug Out / 72
As an Elder sees it – Gone is: / 73
Couch Counsel (formerly note to self) / 74
When I Am, Me / 75
A Breast of a World / 76
Aging, Yet / 78
Acting My Age / 79
For the Second Time / 80
Quicksand / 81
About the Thing / 83
Fix the Pothole Aristotle / 85
Talk on the Trail / 86
Moving In / 87
I Get Everything I Want – Follow Me / 88
My Baba Taught Me Things / 89
Things My Granddaughter Teaches Me / 90
Night Shift / 91
Up from Down / 92
Woman on Earth / 93

## CREATIVE JOURNEY

Because of the Words / 97
Emily Dickinson / 98
Song of Whitman and the Black Man / 99
promise of rainbow / 100
Hot Glass Poem #1 / 101
Hot Glass Poem # 2 / 102

## Acknowledgments / 103

## Author profile / 105

*From the Rim of the Bowl*

# EARTH

*From the Rim of the Bowl*

## Amen to the Park in the North

I am

out on the land

harvesting harmony
part of patterns
in natural movement

circulating all about me
and in me

a loon floats by
as quiet as any moving quiet can be

observing deep
praying deep
giving deep thanks
I still myself
esteem myself

having travelled among the rocks, trees and lakes
my spirit has intertwined equally
with the soft breeze
wind gust
sunshine
bolt of lightning
peace and discord
right in their own right

with strength from superior grace
I gather this life-force of the natural world
I warm to the flow as it penetrates my being
percolates my blood, muscles, bone
like a tincture of medicinal comfort
mends, interlaces, knits, roots me to the earth

soothes to the core

## Dust

we need to go out at night
and look up at the sky

to see the stars
and just witness the cosmic dust
from the comet tail
in orbit swirling around the sun

there is love there

sometimes it may tumble down
too small to notice
and then sometimes
we may feel it
touch our cheek

## Ode to the Raspberry

life has earthquakes
drought and storms
even thorns

watch how weather flips
cruel words can
take flight
from lips

when summer's heat clings to pores
anger soars

after summer rain coolness

under leafy branches
a spot of red
gleams
brightly

sunset like a curve of gold
foils the berry in a crown of glory
this welcome gift brings ecstasy
first of season
recurring for no reason

merry
in your mouth
bursting joy
red raspberry

*Proem: "A shift of sight, like a turnabout a corner,
changes how we see things. It can be redemptive." — Author*

## The Raymond Valley

acid raw despair
from a dreary drizzle
that November kind,
seeps through the windshield
layer into layer

driving to duty
stiffens demeanour
sores the back
such blahs and blahs and no more ha ha's
and I miss summer
mouth droops low
worried that I'm late
I sit tight and straight

around the corner,
like all corners, is a change
a shift of sight
the valley below floats up to my eyes
and like a soothing hand and a "tee-hee-hee"
lifts my chin and lovey-doves my cheek
and the sight of it soars me

zoom zoom the land lays out with
that good space of farm fields
hay bales that roll about and frolic with the curves
along the back tree line
tones of colour like burnt-bush ochre and bashful beige
and hills of orange and tamarack gold
and roasted yam rocks cropping out around greys
and rusty shrubs and pop-up barns
vanilla sheep and caramel horses
that graze unaware of my gaze
at meadows quenched with mist

a look left and right
"Bravo," to the last curtain call
I head straight
Renewed like Mother has stroked
my face with a glove of velour
love passes in front of my eyes
and softness enters my soul
rescued in the Raymond valley

## Ready - Set - Day

the night

which is cold and black
peels back

dark meets dawn
with bird song

the light

in the east
like the start of yeast

rises
stretches
tosses
and catches

big yawn

whistle-ready for it

game on

*Proem: "There is a genius to the stickiness of seeds, telling us that life is meant to take hold of and never let go." — Author*

## Someday in Late Autumn

You leave the city as soon as you can
and head north, parking in the Park

You have planned your day with colour and go for your walk

You notice how clouds wisp white into frilly patches
frayed tapestry against blue sky

If you blink
you might miss the forest wink inviting you to enter

Smelling the softness of leafy earth you breathe it all in

Hearing sounds up ahead
you register the joy of water
bubbling and tumbling over rocks
before you acknowledge the sparkling brook
as if your ears are first
the mind
must wait its turn

In that field ahead
you drink in the happy colour of golden froth
and the milkweed casing waving up
holding sunshine in its cup

You return to your car at dusk
and feel the glow of the lollipop-red sunset
taking the sting out of the air

You know you will be cozy later
remembering the time spent sitting on a barren rock
one day older, gathering up your day, perched in thought
like a favourite sweater to wrap warm around you

*From the Rim of the Bowl*

You eat your snack, drink your water
then glimpse up at twilight wondering how you missed
the curious lone finger that poked a hole in the sky
leaving the afterburn of a moon

You write some words
meditate and stretch
stopping suddenly
to let your eyes take in the kaleidoscope
of a bespangled night sky
that brings you to your knees
make, "Amen,"
and drive homeward
Much later pause long enough
to notice as candlelight
picks up the same multi-coloured flecks of iris
in your lover's eyes

reach out and touch their cheek

We all die someday
yet know you have held infinity
and can take it into eternity

## Eat the Day

Feast your eyes
on delicious dusk
when tender light begins
on Earth's hard-baked crust
and with a loaded brush
all things are stroked
in a buttery hue

this effusive touch
teaches us
to take time out to savour every bite
between first tidbit of dawn
to noonday nibble
up to last quivering swallow before night

having had their fill
out by horizon's backyard
coloured clouds are sent
to gadabout and play
in this perfect light
at the edge of the sky
until
the evening star blows a sweet kiss their way

*Proem: "It is the courageous heart behind the mind, guiding the hand, holding the pen that is mightier than the sword." — Author*

## What the Meek Shall Inherit

We travel to the forest for its canopy
longing to play on the planet's own turf

Deep in the colour of green we are easy
proud of the ache to hug a tree at its girth

We've seen the forest gone from healthy to sick
Yet we know what this planet is worth

We work tirelessly to stop the Blue Meanie
because we are the crew of Spaceship Earth

Sometimes courage comes from fear of doing nothing
Can't we jump from the tower of inconvenient truth

dry our tears from an ocean of struggle
come out swinging for what 'He' promised
to us at birth

*From the Rim of the Bowl*

# YOUNG WOMEN

*From the Rim of the Bowl*

## Infamous Eve

Languishingly leaning
over-top Adam's neon-coloured handle bars
she suddenly holds him
with her pretty, pink-popsicle-cool mouth
takes with her tiny beaded drops
the sunshine made above his chin
leaves him off-balance
blinking "Oh Oh Oh" from his eyes
and a bubble glistening in the corner of his goofy grin.

Pretending not to stare
Tracy, Sarah and Chris
shift, shrug and sit back
against the shady school brick waiting to copy her homework
studying her squint walking back as if nothing's amiss
and Adam's "Look-no-hands" dart down Daredevil Hill
silver spokes streaking
his "Whahoo!"
ringing in their ears
registering silently that Eve knows how to kiss.

## **Puddle bridge**

deep into the park
her innocence coming back
slow but coming
then suddenly
up ahead a frozen puddle
the colour of computer-monitor-turned-off

pupil-scope sent out
returns
A-okay
puddle-glacious

she runs up
ssllllllliiiiiiiiiiiiiddes across

blinking back
memories
bridge back to past
before braces
clavichordial row of crooked ivories
before they looked
before they stared
before they touched

emotion heaved out and up
into absorbent sky

ice cracks
bringing
sinking
stomach flutter
up-then-across
like an elevator catching its floor
snowbank-safe on the other side

she promises
to come back
for her thoughts are saved in all-surround forest

*From the Rim of the Bowl*

and the puddle
trusting only it
to bridge her gap

## Gimme Lights

her neck stretches out the car window
her glee seems to announce
"Gimme those lights"

words and warnings
arguing and questioning
back and forth
stay or go
gone
and who can blame her

trading the brown of home and hearth
for the glow of yellow filaments
trusting only in the glory of youth and mirth
trusting only in shallow beauty and glamour

during the next years of keen and cunning
amassing fancy toys and fashion
and everything in a 'brand' name
battles to be won
hail the struggle to the top
and the promise of money and fame and glory

"but be careful" echoes in her ears

in the throat now wearing a lump
finding out
that so many alliances
like so many appliances
end up in the city dump

## Nana – Look and See

I search for music to slit my wrists by
but no band will play
it hurts to feel the feelings
hammers pound night and day
it's dog eat dog yet I should be grateful
I have everything you say
won't lick your hand
don't want this stuff
can't be your kind of gay
sun comes up
I run for cover every damn, damn day
Can't stop the crush
sometimes it bursts
sometimes it sprays
you can't see what I can't handle
I'm burying it my way
can't make it stop not you — not them
get it okay?

on your race down the highway
on to EM Recovery bay
a cop pulls you over
and he listens
lets you go on your way
it happens he says sadly
seen it day after day after day
his warning echoes in your ear
that I might do it one day

my demons don't seem real to you
they poke and prod
I'm prey
I'm numb to all your warnings
I'm cursed — I'll pay
For me I think of how to end it
maybe some day
for me you quote the bible
for me you'll pray

## Child – Look and See

I can't believe my ears
when your mom cried out the news.
You tried again to kill yourself
picked the wrists to abuse.
I don't get it.
Don't you see you're lucky,
one of the very few?

You hurt me.
What could be your problem?
Give me a clue.

The Internet – those groups can take you down –
so Boo Hoo.
Turn it all off and go outside or
give a good book its due.
I lack for words but I have my heart
and trust in you.
Okay, end of lecture, but here's the scoop anew.

I was young, remember bullies, heartache, hormones — phew!

Don't want to harp.
I see your ache so will quickly tell you true.
These things will pass.
It happens to all of us,
a rocky avenue.
But try to see what I am saying.

I made it through.

So can you.

## You may become aware

during the festivity around the new mother
who is beaming
as she plays with Baby Joy

that there is another woman in the corner
who watches
as a beggar tries to taste food
long fingers clenched
body pressing emaciation against the store window display

since despite every test, treatment, trusted advice
she has failed to fill up the womb

and you come to understand through whispers
how her husband without
a knock
was suddenly in the bathroom doorway
unsuccessful at camouflaging
concern
pleas from his parents looming
as he presses her
and she responds
with a microscopic shake of her obedient head

her eyes pleading
his sterile look out
and you grasp the significance
of this morning's ruin
the unwelcome stain
and fate of their union

## It Stands Still for Her

you can say it can't
but it can

stand still

when her moan is loud
when her moan is long
her contractions
not far apart now
her breathing hard
her panting strong
her struggle to breathe out
her pushing
everyone knows it's coming
boy or girl

time

it moves on
for everyone in the room

but not for the mother
not until
she hears, "It's healthy."

## Roommates

I splash my face, a warm-water ritual, and look up
at eyes happy with the new day and hair wet on the edges
as though all night had been one of rapture,
steaming loins and love spent
As if that ever happens
I bow my head and heed his voice from above
What-time-is-it-I'm-going-to-be-late-is-the-coffee-ready?

I flip the visor down to check my lipstick, then my hair — all still good
eyes sparkle, lips stretch wide with the recent memory of purchases
I got everything on the list but
gaze turns down when next I hear
What-took-you-so-long-I'm-bored-did-you-get-me-anything?

After the long hike, I wash my hands of good clean dirt then chin up
my face returns a deep-dreamy peacefulness,
pink roses in my cheeks
remembering every solid treasure in every new path taken
My heart drops, listening to
Where-were-you-what-do-you-see-in-that-park-anyway-
what's-for-dinner?

Eyes peer around the corner, surprised that feet follow
and then the words just before the slam of the door,
I'm-leaving-you-ciao-oh-and-by-the-way-I'm-taking-the-mirrors.

## Guilt on the Menu

*"Marilyn Monroe, once, wore a dress that was so tight, someone said that she must have been poured into it, with a quart and a half to spare. She was an iconic sex symbol, curves everywhere, but by today's media standards, she would be considered fat."*
*— Author unknown*


Obesity, Fat Girl and Chubby sit together in the lunch room
waiting
hoping
for Bones, Twig Bitches and Anorexia to sit at their table

but watch them
go past them
heading for where the cool boys beckon

one table eats, quietly brushing off damage, swallowing shame
one table snickers, swallowing giggles, brushing on blame

later, much later and older

meanness doesn't sit anywhere
doesn't pierce the air
not anymore

some meet at the table of forgive and forgetness
some take a seat with brooding and bitterness

lunch still is lunch

## Gotta Have It Once a Month
## Green Dream Jelly Bean

Slipping past lips
seals the fate
of the candy-coated bullet
a captive carried on a slippery current.
The executioner tongue
takes up the innocent bean
feels it clicking its protest
against white enamel
subdues and
guides it into masticating molars.
A guilty green sent to the guillotine.

Glucose explodes to the roof
gushing granules
gliding gritty over gums.

A final chop jogs the jelly
jiggles loose a spearmint full-flavoured flood
and makes sucking wet air and
thrusting slurps down the throat
lap-luscious.

A dextrose dream fit for any Queen.

*From the Rim of the Bowl*

# SNOW

*From the Rim of the Bowl*

## Winter Menu

In the field
last night's snow
reminds me of my Grandma saying, "Mornin', Hon"
as I watch her lay out a fresh tablecloth.
See where the deer has walked.
It's like that dribble of wine stain that didn't wash out.

Back in the wood,
golden beech leaves, crunchy collections in the nook of a tree
beckon like a basket of crusty rolls. Bring on the butter.

On the pond
a white-covered scoop of beaver lodge
is served like a side-order of mashed
with creamy drifts.

Today's special is hearty red granite
in moist and meaty chunks.
Pass the salt and pepper.

Thawed from the morning sunshine
broccoli green moss peeks out
from under flowerets of frost.

Along the creek
frozen root beer froth
and tea-coloured trickles
candy-stage brittle
look finger-licking sweet.

I turn back.
My snowshoe tracks
like taking a friend's hand
lead me home.

I know dinner's waiting.
Sure I'll eat
but I'm already full.

## Snow Glitterati

It's a soft wet snow that sticks as if to say
"Time for fresh makeup
set the stage
everyone make way."

From the window I see that even the clouds
are sent away.
Starting out the front door
the walkway is now a runway.

Velvet sky adhering
bright lights appearing
all gleaming
all glamour
all flash.
Lawn fresh white for an autograph
from that new kid
and that puddle
making a splash.

There's a crowd of spruce trees
as the sun dips about
or maybe it's a huddle of little girl legs
in party dresses
glimmering
shimmering
admiring their tresses.

I wonder what they're gossiping about
waiting for the stars to come out.

## Made You Look

in spring I am but big twigs and branches
tangling up your sky of blue
in summer I am a mesh of leaves
soft light and dark green
in fall I create a cover-up
of colours
you'll be in need of a rake
in early winter you may deplore
my bare and lean soggy shape

then comes snow to freshen your focus

introducing you to the real me

with powder-laden limbs you clearly see who I am
different am I not
from that other tree and that one

my boughs and limbs in detail
my poke-about branches
my trunk a silhouette
inked against the atmosphere
these are my marks
and like your fingerprints
they distinguish me from others

presenting to you

my unique tree-ness

*Proem: "I believe that if you strive for peace and you find peace then you are less likely to disturb the peace of others. — Author*

## White Silence

During mellow reveries while trudging through the snow,
each snowshoe must lift, push and pump from the heart,
a clear mind can analyze, assemble, collect and compile
with the intensity of some philosopher like that of Diderot
the excellent whispered thoughts of Dante, Swift,
Voltaire and Rousseau.

Perchance to find embedded an image of artistic display,
like frozen doily designs around a wet icy pool
framed by otter's slide patterns; nature saturates deep inside.
If exhausted by quest and nothing left to say
miles far off, watching evening shadows begin their lengths,
ideas by Pythagoras, Descartes, Pascal and Pope enlighten the way.

Content with day's search for more frontier space to unfold
and turning to follow the trail home
using steady quiet rhythm of working body parts,
a state of white silent meditation — the only goal
whether under grey skies, sunshine or moonlit night
simply clinging to the process, nurtures and heals my solitary soul.

## Big Dollop for the Town Tailor

It's lookin' like time to pick cotton

Last night has sent a big dollop onto the face of my town park.
Lazy sun melts it slowly,
leaving cursive script hanging from limb to limb
and Dali-esque clocks draped over bars of the iron gate.

Soft and mellow on the old stump it sits a giant marshmallow.

The gazebo fence railing looks like fresh dough
that was left to rise
now double in size
ready to punch down and shape into loaves.

The branch of the big white pine
holds its arm straight out
cotton-sleeved
as though waiting to be measured for a new suit.

## Joy of the Snowfall

there is bliss
in every speck of whiteness around you
soft
wet
white
falling from white
sticking to white
cool zest
simple
joy
will open your heart and then prance in

if you let it
this dot of emotion in your heart can magnify 1000 times

you might explode
but you try to hold in your breath
for fear of losing your body

if you inhale too deeply
your whole being may disperse
and re-enter as a field of swirling cosmic dust

yet you do inhale inwards
as far as you can

and when you come out of that
you restrict the sweet feeling
while holding your mouth closed

you bond just so
wrapping in your humanity
by letting your lips stretch across
but still squeezing
they form
a smile
that feels as wide as a mile
until the sweetness flows

dives down and out
through your toes

you are glad for being
a physical being
grateful to be blessed
with the rawness and rapture of human essence
a capacity to feel glorious

you can store the moment
in your special space
where there is always
more room for joy

go ahead
let it dance right in

## Poof

snow's since melted in the woods

you scan the land
dead of colour
except for brown
and variations
depending on where the light gets in

then pop pop pop
you swear you hear them
calling out
left then right
"Look at me me me"
Lady's Slippers
"Suivez moi jeune fille," pink, purple, plump,
purely provocative

you steady your legs
your craving

awake
stirred

keep walking

with an appetite for more

*From the Rim of the Bowl*

## **We See Music**

we peel back our cardboard flaps
before traffic beeps and honks

sun's pop over peaceful city
shines on jack-frosty sidewalks
quickly melts the snow-dusting on chocolate earth
a classic night when the weather didn't win
a night when the snow didn't come in

noon snow collects on shrubs
heavy like giant eye-lashes curling over
cold, clean, country-fresh joy rushes in
a day with lots of hot water
a day when the socks all matched

slip, hop and sit
we'll tough it out
we'll try for coins

we hear enough of them jingle
for a loaf of bread or ...
then let's rock

wind blows sleet
into evening head-lights
jazzy snow babidadiboppadoo
we meander through
and make a million wishes by midnight

morning shock
it's a flock of flakes
three duvets high
a lofty hush
they are stuck
they must stay home
a pillow for our blues-weary souls
we'll rise up
we'll climb

*From the Rim of the Bowl*

we'll cheer
and applaud

how
a city can quiet itself

## In October's Cool Climate

I watch gusts of wind stir up the terrain before me. Whorls of maple and oak leaves take off like a frightened flock of shorebirds. I ask the wind questions. Why have all the trees lost their leaves except the beech? Why does each leaf shimmer in the fading light in its own gold foil as though clinging to memories of sun-soaked days?

In November, the calendar tells me winter is coming. Yet the farmer up the road tells me, "Tamarack trees still have their buds." The warm chocolate-brown earth glistens with the few flakes of snow like a cake still warm melting the first layer of icing. Nimbus clouds heave up across the horizon like alabaster breasts catching the final gaze of the sun as it winks goodnight. I can tolerate the chill in the air.

In December, at dusk, I stop to admire the natural, outdoor art exhibition in the town park; the snow hangs in the twigs of hemlock like exotic sea-fan coral swaying beauty. The beech leaves hang on. Their branches wave at me like the many arms of belly dancers, dangling golden gems. I can savour my small-town street, swept clean with lamplight. It takes away the sting in the air.

In January, the chickadees land on the feeder, feathers fluffed up against the cold, their little twig feet looking like one false move and they'll snap. My arms ache from snow- shoveling. Raspberry bushes are curled over, mascara heavy. The forecast of minus 30 below is pushed away with the friendly invitation to a hot-tub party. I step down into the water, heat enveloping my body the way an old glove feels familiar, the leather warming up around the memory of shape.

In February, I slide under the covers and sink into despair.
A dreary morning forecast announces more winter. All I can smell is wet mitts and wet dog. Looking out the window at the snow land laid out before me reminds me of my eight-year-old efforts to make my bed, trying to mimic my mother's skilled hands at smoothing lumps out of white sheets.

In March, the beech leaves shake against a worn white background like a jangle of coins about to wear out cotton threads of a pants pocket. The sun shines on plump raindrops clinging along my backyard clothes line, turning it into a diamond necklace strung out, until a passing cloud on silent tip-toe snatches it away. I study the poplar trees, living breathing trunks; black silhouettes soaked with cold, crocheting their branches as though they have resolved to stay warm together.

In April, along the salt-caked muddy roadway the snowplow leaves layers of wedding cake design in its path. I treasure the cozy fireplace, the warmth of loving arms and kissing willing lips. In the morning my boot presses down on thin ice, making sounds like ice cubes tinkling in a glass, a toast to spring. The warm rays of afternoon sun on my cheek are as welcome as lover's breath. In the strawberry-kissed dusk a breeze purrs a peaceful prayer.

In May, the Farmer's Almanac predicts a good year. The strong sun reminds the earth to soften and prepare for new growth. And then the beech leaves, with a puff of air, twirl and drop gently to the ground, carbon-coloured suits coated in faith.

I feel their presence gone and I, too, feel the chill finally leave my soul.

# LOVE AND OTHER THINGS

*From the Rim of the Bowl*

## Sarajevo

I wonder why I chose this city
this rainy night,
this street now deserted

then I see you walking towards me
with a look that says, "I like you," in any language

puddle fun beneath me
my feet splashing
you are laughing.

I feel a hunger for oneness
like lovers sleeping
and hear the joy of church bells ringing
those peaceful voices inside singing.

But I spot the bullet holes
in the walls of the cathedral
then a sudden tip-tapping
drips go flinging
and we're strangers passing.

I'm left with
that hollow sound.

I'll always wonder
in lonely reminiscing.
It was only our umbrellas kissing.

## I Know Nothing About Tides

my house
lies on bedrock
once out the door
my feet feel firmness
that kind of solidity
that once you made love on — you never forget

was invited to the east coast
years ago
I drove
my friends didn't prepare me for the shock
tide was out
winced at the raw red earth — a wound — hurt if you touched it
but good potatoes

I learned in Geography
that tides are commanded to ebb and flow
teacher never explained why
it's like a dog whose master doesn't want it to follow
points a finger, "Go home."

now I'm in the middle of the country where I read a story about
the west coast tide and the current — Lucifer
let it carry a girl out to sea
no moon, the fog be-devilling her mind
safety uncertain
fate unknown
her future in the hands of bioluminescence
and blades of kelp
streaming radiant arrows

and I spellbound
until she sees that this is a clue, the direction of the moving kelp
showing which way to turn
for her
the way back
and finally she feels
the stability

and hush
of water-smoothing pebbles

was she naked?
now I want to see the west coast
I get in the car and drive.

*From the Rim of the Bowl*

## **HEY**

He must raise an empty glass
try waving
snapping fingers
and shouting

"HEY?"

She has but to lean over
elbows pressing inwards
her bosom
doing the calling for her

*"HEY BARTENDER!"*

## Tune of Words

Echo of the slammed door
beats against my soul

remembering
you tried to break good will
your will over mine

I get up for rum and ice
refresh my solitude
up the volume
knees hugged tight
secure my attitude

like favourable winds
that reverse weather
I feel your shy presence at the door

my lips tight shrinking failure

ruin

until invisible fingers squeeze
your Adam's apple
and out comes

the healing
"I'm sorry," tune

## Bright Morning Thoughts

Looking for the right one
why go to great pains?
Some people have skyscraper IQ's.
Some don't have any brains.

Why search for a 'slim', a 'stunning' and 'tall'?
Not a chance for winner-take-all.

Why squander time hunting for talent, money or song?

I must remember these crisp thoughts at dawn.

I could accept who I am, stay away from the bar,
spot the one who thinks he loves me, so far.

He's been right under my nose,
sees the 'good' in me, I suppose.

I say we cook up a stew,
with enough savoury sauce it will feed two.
The next day there's meat
and potatoes from storage.
There's a dozen ways to tip-top porridge.
We can grow into love,
build on it day by day.

There's enough sweet wind to sail away.
We can feed some kids.
In fact let's have a brew.
I love you I do.
I'll tell you too.

## Love Gamble

First nice day to sit out
winter world has gone to slush
skin cells make merry
under sun's rays
brain cells turn to mush
brightness penetrates her eyelids
as if an old guy's tipped his hat
leave her alone
let her sleep
just what are you looking at?

there is this guy
a-kind-of-a-friend
with promise of new shine
four strong walls if she wants them
life of flowers, song and wine
been so cold that her mind is set
tugs her back to hibernate
old seasons of poverty
lies'n cheatin'
seem to dictate her fate

her body could choose to stand
go over'n pick up that rake
could plant some seeds
then sit'n watch 'em take
she sees that hoe's come-hither look
her gamble to take
then watch that garden grow
and keep
what no winter dare take

## Spaces

No bridge can span the gulf between us
after words freeze-dry and crash in mid-glare.

We stand on pedestals of anger
directing disdain through the air.

Then you say, "Honey, we need to talk."
The space between us turns small.

Wrapped in a hug, we hold on tight
until there's no space between us at all.

When you tease until I crack a smile,
shooting stars fly across my breasts.

Barely a beat between I love you I love you too.
True feelings have passed another test.

## Listen to You

If for months you haven't sold work
you feel bad but it's perhaps not that, which really bugs you.
It's probably that nobody ever really listens.

You may retreat
where your kitchen hands make steam, shave, pare, pulp
membrane,
strip, ration, peal, layer and seal,
remembering how
you told the school board that they shouldn't have hotdog days
and you told the municipal board that they shouldn't cut down
that 300-year-old tree.
No one ever pays attention.

It's your anniversary.
He
comes home. You see him smiling and winking.
He didn't forget to buy bread, milk and batteries.

Later, if you ever take note, you might
register the sound
of how loud-like is the little cry you utter
while you're having a really intense orgasm flat out
where you try to hold down the volume
hold down your humanity
and it sneaks out
just barely audible yet full of meaning.
You think that they
must
have heard it
right through
to the other side of the earth.

## Mistress

he makes reservations
she agrees to meet for dinner-talk
but refuses to hold his hand walking from the parking lot

he looks at the half-moon against a thin black sky
like a 'Holy' wafer snapped in two

she glances up from the menu
empty flavour of doubt
but only for a moment
reluctance to patch things up her fault
a dark frozen glare
a convoluted stare
waiting to escape, her fingernail doodles,
trail around a cold cocktail glass
'Jack Frost' against midnight
tangled licorice-whips in the foggy mass

he wonders what happened and misses
those 'God but you're wonderful' kisses

she cites irreconcilable differences
she seeks joint custody of their son
and then she says, "We're done."

her eyes droop
her mouth forms a yawn
pale lips buckle in dryness shrinking closure
then she's gone

his sad heart on the ground
the 'other guy' has won

## You are in love

with yourself
for the rest of your life
at least for tonight
it's been a long, lonesome road, humdrum and hard,
dull and doubtful
tedious and tiresome but
after rehearsals, re-dos, reworks, rewrites, repaints,
you get applause, awards, laughs, book signings, sales,
this is good
you are good
sacrifice was worth it
energy comes
flows, fluffs, soars and somersaults up to the top

nothing can turn down your inner light
un-shimmer your shimmer
lower the level of your lumens
no drug or drink can lay you low
you can't possibly sleep but who wants to?
from inside you kiss yourself, congratulate, cheer, praise
squeeze your whole being
put a crown on your head
keep it on
spin around and glow
glow
glow

## Beautiful Black

once upon a time we could see night as it was meant to be black,
tired, we slid our skin under skins
eyes open
as light dimmed it held down our limbs
relaxed, nothing to be brave about
anonymous black
commenced descent

in lap of obscurity, indistinct lover
fetching sweetness
twinkled and sprinkled
sifted and drifted
hovered and covered
wrapped and packeted

dawn far to come
our impatience numb
we savoured the nothingness
yet fancied the fullness
the void and the thatness
of beautiful blackness

*From the Rim of the Bowl*

# ELDERS

*From the Rim of the Bowl*

## Benefit of Within

Casting off

the sole crew
towards your internal sea
surfing waves of spiritual space
you take yourself into the centre of your temple

In the cathedral of your mind
you cruise your cerebral church
In the splendor of your soul
you sail searching peace
Within the walls of your heart
you explore your personal worth

You pick up pieces of discarded dreams
sweeten sour thoughts
plunge and scrub clean harsh words
glue back broken caresses
blink away blackness
and take time to re-savour rushed-through flavour

Sensing life secure you arrow forth
unsnarl from mortal coils
and drop into golden gossamer hands
Speaking to your god in your own way
you hear the value of blessed treasures spreading you generous
You see a table in a sun-drenched field
for gathered friends
There is something for everyone
that each one especially likes

The shutter clicks
imprinting enrichment
Airy thoughts inflate and bubble
catching an upward current
You feel the softness of rebirth

Refreshed

*From the Rim of the Bowl*

feeling bigger than whole
from the inside you kiss yourself alert
wave bye on the other shore of prayer
that you can cross every day.

## Slow Cooker

carrots in the community garden
first-frosted under your feet
dug up before the snow flies
makes them tasty and sweet

into the crock pot after plenty scrubbing
with taters, onions, broth
spices do a do-si-do in the cooker
turned out better than you thought.

next day's taste improved again
since
juices have swapped flavours
and it's heaven in a bowl
so you invite over the neighbours
who remark upon the earthiness
know what it is to savour
home-made goodness
and the ambiance
and appreciate your labour

## You Know That You're Not Really Important

the main road was blocked
landslide
you find yourself up in the mountain because of the detour

somewhere away from the tourist areas
hungry

you know that
by the look on the young girl's face
the tip was too big
rationalize it by
'it was good pizza'

the girl walks back to stand under the kitchen stone archway
you smile at her and her friend
at the giggles

her friend shouts something

you give your head a shake
your Hermès scarf blowing in the cool breeze
you don't understand the language
you lift one hand eyes asking

the waitress says
"She dreams, one day, of being you."

you take in a breath of astonishment
shoulders shrug
lips smile
button up your faux-fur fall coat

you climb up the hill
hand in a pocket
grab at the key bob
and click to unlock
hear, "Beep"
and hear them in unison, "Ooohh."

*From the Rim of the Bowl*

you stand
you catch your breath
you get in the car
then drive
dreamily being you

## Eyes Bug Out

at the kitchen window
gazing out
my only aim
I spied a bug and quickly pushed it against the pane

bumpy under my finger
feeling its hard shell
I tried to crush it further but didn't do very well

how dare it spoil my reverie
I flung it to the sink
under dirty dishes it slipped down the brink
I think
turning on the faucet
commanding it down the drain
I thought this is my house
I
the higher organism shall remain

pouring out my superior liquid roast
after fetching my morning paper
I noted
news not bad
on the whole
up and up
then looked down

and saw 'Bug' calmly treading in my cup

## As an Elder sees it — Gone is:

Pure as Mountain Air
Naturally Good
Sweet Wind
Clean Water
Brook Trout
April Fresh
Wilderness
Clear Sky

Absolute Silence
Old Forest
Pristine Sea
Right as Rain
Land of Plenty
White as Snow
This Good Earth

and gone are

Brave Hearts

or

Are you there?

## Couch Counsel (formerly note to self)

I look down
I shudder
the bug had been at my leg
for what must have been an hour
and now it's done its sucking
much too full
to fly away

we count on webs
that glue
confine
arrest
entrap
catch pests is what arachnids do
snare
those maddening things
that bite
by spinning out their mighty might

I give my head a hasty shake
recall how earlier this day
I swept aside
that silken lace
thoughts now wiser
kinder
I should not have killed the spider

## When I Am, Me

I am five. There are many questions, some answers, some are cruel.
I decide
I will hide who I really am.
I'm out of love. I'm out of energy. I'm out of faith, hope and charity.
I'm out for myself.

I am twenty-five, gasping in loneliness, grasping for courage
that doesn't come. Hope passes through holes of my soul.

I am thirty-five. I am solid. I have collected enough me-points
to buy a door.
I risk. I open. I find I am not the sole one.

I am sixty-five. I am grateful I let someone in.
I am thankful for faith, hope, charity and love.

I am eighty-five. I am alone. I regret nothing.
Myself is saved. I will someday die,
my energy out there.

## A Breast of a World

Starting out as naked no-shapes, wee cry to sky
baby-soft network
hungry for a nipple not her own, found without eye
soon is toddler tumbling bump-p-p-ity
recognized within wailing instant
picked up, forgotten and buried against deep-bosomed generosity
in a blink girlish glee playing dress-up, red-lipped makeup
in wink, à la lace, in a 'twinkling' à la 'cleavage'
push-up, à la va-va-va-voom
stealing looks from everyone in the room

under burning gaze, warm dough rises
contact with fire, altering elemental anatomy
cupped for first kiss against whiskered lips' sweet-rough reality
triggering body quakes, leaving radiating pleasure
telescopic tingling firmed in their wake

then mountains out of mole-hills
heaves and valleys on course
soft mewling lips against bursting faucets, cocooned purpose
quenching thirst

eventual shift in axis
fading, sagging, callous puppetry played by gravity
maniacal moods maniacal menses maniacal menopause
dominant orbs casting swollen spells over any cause
sudden crisis a lump that can't be swallowed
allowing medical intervention
left with mammary mangled hollow

and slowing down
feeling the ever of never never-dom
hope capsized, mimic martyrdom
now, pretty daughter mocks her mother's mammary manual
daily bawl or brawl, must strive to think like sage
but daughter disappears, taking out the door perky profile,
the best page

what emotions clashed, then tearless quiet
where memories of who, when, why are rehashed
final twist, overview over last night's bouquet
cool, pale, languished bloom of grace approaching shapeless
dropped, dew-robbed, petal against the hospital sheet
rest-place.

## Aging, Yet

on my face
are lines so bold
wisdom streams from every fold

aspirations have been high
I'm told
but success I have
riches
I hold

Yet

from the jar of what-to-do today
Granddaughter picks my arm to play

she grabs a marker
just to tease

connect the dots of age spots

aww — please

## Acting My Age

The public park is past its lush
heated through
cooked, roasted, grilled, fried, baked
surface lost its elasticity, like me
Finger tips
trace and retrace folds on my face
my time on earth written in Braille

Yet another autumn
yet another path
I stop to watch
a hawk carried up by a current of air
rise then drop
then sweep upwards again
seemingly drifting without purpose
like the floater caught in an updraft
across my eye

In the end I stand under a tree
on a medley of leaves
crispy crumble on the forest floor
waiting
for that chickadee
to come closer
I invite it
careful not
to appear eager
so it won't know how much I want it
to be my friend

One day
I too will be dust on the path
memories for the chickadee

## For the Second Time

the mother yells
one of her daily drudged-up duteous drawls
rehearsed since some Sixties show.
With her head tilted up towards the stairs
her voice cracks on the "school" part of
"Hurry up Pumpkin you'll be late for ..."

"Schoooooool" mocks the older son, her dropout.
Then he hides a smirk behind a bite of buttery toast,
knowing indifference will bounce back her glare
which will then fall on the daughter, the one without a shell.
She imagines her mother sees the loss of virginity
in the sore at the raw corner of her mouth.
Not until elbows melt off the edge of the table
does she sense her gaze move off her case.

Taking a distant look she momentarily dips into her mother's space,
imagines, feels and subconsciously
imprints herself
with future pain.
She watches how repeatedly rinsed and squeezed
under wrinkled hands
the kitchen cloth sweeps clean
earnest expectations
like those recurring crumbs left on the counter.

## Quicksand

the app was free for 30 days
curious of course
she started
with a simple genealogy search
and saw that
after the Great War
her grandmother immigrated
as a young girl

Document notation
"released to int. husband"
and
under the column heading, Religion,
it was noted
"can read and write Hebrew"

what did it mean?
could it mean?

she turned her head
away from the screen
and
started to sink
and
wanted to move her feet
but
she was trapped

the sand up to her knees
quick to her waist
rough along her chin
grit in her mouth
filling her nose
scratching at her eyes
she made the sign of the cross
like they were taught in the new church
the new world

*From the Rim of the Bowl*

she knew about the Holocaust
she has seen the t-shirts 6MWE
she heeds the warning

her breathing
is different now

## About the Thing

The thing
about the thing is
how fast it grew
like a snowball
pushed off the top of a hill
gathering
amassing light
glowing white
more weight
mounting
no stopping it
then an important person said
it was important
and people marveled at it

some sang songs
some prayed
some wrote poetry
and some had so much to praise
that they filled a book

some countries identified their own worth
with its importance
some were so attracted to this devotion
this radiant power
they dropped
to their knees in prayer and more prayer

then the thing grew bigger and bigger and
blew up
destroyed before our eyes
ripping and tearing as it went
we felt the pain
wanted it to stop
wanted someone to put it back together
but authorities said that it was too risky to operate

some believe that this thing will come back

some are left
to live out their lives
with shrapnel
in their souls

## Fix the Pothole Aristotle

Your 'HIS'story of the world
like you created it yourself
didn't include us
lording over everything, ruling, giving orders
gold-plated annals with tales of wars and glories

pressure to subdue women

press her into a mold
of your liking

a woman made you
you rise above her?

I don't think so
women
make the world go round
grow it, feed it, clothe it and keep it on the right path

you forget we are here
on the same road

we remind you of it — feel the crack
in your pavement? resurface

we add to the story — feel that rut
in your road? smooth the groove

we spread our worth — feel the hazards
of the hairpin curves? straighten out

our strength in numbers — feel the wobble
on your pedestal? move over

oh ... and on the march
to match economic empowerment?

fix the pothole Aristotle

## Talk on the Trail

There is a beat from placing one foot in front of the other.
Questions pound out like a drum from your heart.
Will he walk? Will she get better? Will they marry?
Will they get back together?

Next come the skip-a-beats,
would have, might have, could have, should have.
Then comes get-this-quick-out-of-the-way talk.
He will make it. She'll be fine. They'll do their best.
All they can do is try.

The answers crisp up like muffin tops
in the last five minutes of baking.
You'll help where you can.

There's a place on the path where you forget yourself.
You may hear the crow at any time. It's a different spot each day.
Despair slides down and off.

Chatter from your brain comes to a halt so you can hear
the real talk in your head. Being human
is quieted to the size of a chickadee's heart
with a huge sense of belonging to life.

Now with each breath out
you relax until you go moss-deep.

With a tilt of the head back you connect
to the blue sky. A hawk drifts into view. You watch it suddenly drop
then carry on up, a current with unknown direction,
the same way a floater drops then lifts across your line of sight.

Turning to go home you face your age.

One day you will die, leave the earth and lose it all,
or
you will gain a universe.

## Moving In

there are different neighbours today
I shake hands with many a new face
chock-full
of appeasing immigrant smile
hoping
that innocence is enough

but across the street
terror stiffens a family's features
those new faces with long noses
are not known
chunks of coal for nostrils
are not known
skin like layers of smoke under the dermis
are not known

I'm curious what I might find
seeing they are a humble kind
others not so sure
aren't as secure
fear of difference
endures

there are some to blame
news reports focus on negative imaging
scripts and films depict them menacing
shameless game
only the 'Media' can change the legacy

those who fear need to see
some good in all
they ought to be shown
these things are well known

*Proem: "A good life is about how many times you laughed your guts out." ~Alfred Engerer*

## I Get Everything I Want — Follow Me

Be strong. Strong is a word, not strong enough.
Be happy. Happy is a word, not happy enough.
Be Strong Happy. That is clear.
Get everything you want.
That's what it's about. Isn't it? Then you'll be Strong Happy.
There is a catch.
You can't want the shallow.
Aim for the deep.
When you have family, friends and laughter
and love is there
everywhere about you and inside you
then
you will have Strong Happy.
Nothing can get you down.
That's right.
You know it.
When your niece tells a joke at the dinner table
and gives the punch line just as you take a gulp of beer
and you laugh spraying suds everywhere and nobody cares
that is Strong Happy.

Your soul calls out, "Ohhhhh yesssss."
The best of you is right here right now.
You have everything.
I saw you. You took notes. Strong Good.

*Proem: "Vulgar human nature at its most impulsive vantage point is that of perceived righteousness." — Author*

## My Baba Taught Me Things

When her English didn't work,
I remember once my dainty grandmother
my Baba
closing the front door
on certain people
leaving them with a good Slavic phrase
which roughly means, "I hope a dog shits on your head."

I remember how I admired her candour.
It dawned on me that I really should learn the language
of the old country.

I think about the men that came today with chainsaws
for a snowmobile trail behind my backyard.

I watched the leader
build prefab walls of arrogance
while he stopped his hand inches away
from itching his crotch.

I remember how he boasted, "This means jobs. It's been approved."
Then he told me, "You can't do nothing,"
while he ordered his men to take down the forest canopy.

I roughly said, "Pas ti posra na glavu,"
and left.

At least the day wasn't a total loss.

## Things My Granddaughter Teaches Me

She is now four years old.
She is eating her cereal the same way she eats life.
She takes it all in with a high degree of drama,
gobbling — chomping — slurping.
I have finished my cereal but watching how she enjoys hers
makes me hungry again.

She scrapes the rim of the bowl.
She suddenly stops and stares at me
aware, that I am watching her.

Careful to push her long hair out of the way
she then takes in a quick breath.
She says, like she really needs to tell me to explain,
"I left some of the bits up on the side
for later, for the crunch, when I want some crunch."

I say, "Someone once said, that you really only ever taste
the first and the last
bite of every meal."

Her eyes go round, "That's so sad, Baba."
"You're right," I say then I lean over and give her a little kiss.

## **Night Shift**

In the wee hours you can't sleep, can't close your eyes.
You stare out
at velour blackness.
Some say, "It's those horrible 3 AM's of the soul that writers have."
Lamentable — No —
Floating in a leisurely darkness
between pillow and ear is your cozy softness.

Demand of dawn and duty still hours to go,
whispers of "Stay awake" emanate from feathers below.
You allow your mind's reunion with dust and paper, letter and word.

Your life,
like a library, lays out before you,
adventures inside your head, and not with woe
you give equal attention to friend and foe.

Digging deep into titles stacked on old shelves
you re-file facts in your reference section,
recite poetry
pour over picture books
skip the ghost stories
caress the classics
puzzle over mysteries
and open up to fantasy.
With every toss and turn you hear "Pick me, pick me."

Innocence long gone
or reconciled,
you wander over a wealth of journeys
romantic, comedic, tragic or wild

stories
you could never have known as a sleepy child.

## Up from Down

Taking in a prayer breath
giving my hope some air
day-dreams surface fat and jolly
and take away the melancholy.

As sadness leaves a gnawing gap
part of me tries to grab sad back
but I wrestle it on
give it wings
until the hole inside me fills and sings.

## Woman on Earth

she is under the
syndrome's spell
yes she is

she does the yelling
she does the crying
every month

is accused of being grouchy
her breasts are tender
nipples brushing under the inside of her shirt
uncomfortable while at the same time
pleasurable
but there is this need for action
to do something
there is power with these waves — these cycles
the strongest power in the world
the time the womb is getting ready
to be doing what needs to be done
Hah!
then days later
especially with women in sync

you think
you might try to stop us
during that after-the-menstrual-cycle wave
with progesterone juicing through our veins
never
we will not be bullied
not lie down and quiver
not cave in
not be defeated

our plan is a plan of action
a big fight
save the green
save Planet Earth
it's like war

but a woman's way of war
doing battle on our own terms
day by each time-of-the-month day
connected in our rhythms

women have made a lot happen
the women's movement is one of the most
successful revolutions
sweeping change
women aren't afraid
of change
women are agents of change

older women have wisdom
older women will act as advisers
women when empowered can act over those
who choose to hurt the environment
and hurt each other
as they wage destructive war
those who choose to harm the planet
will not realize that the battles
by women
will come in cycles
the small
then the large
then the super battles
an accumulation of offensive moves
those who choose to harm the planet
will not be able to explain the manoeuvres
women like us will know the strategy of the tides
the ebbs and the flows
waves that eventually erode the huge beast
and it is all part of the plan

Earth's luck is about to change

*From the Rim of the Bowl*

# CREATIVE JOURNEY

*From the Rim of the Bowl*

## Because of the Words

As he spoke
I know this poet
knew me
or so I hoped

upon hearing them
the words drew me into their tide
a wondrous draw down deep
I went for the dive
somewhere inside I gulped
somewhere outside I glowed
from the truth of them

for a long while
I sat in the warmth of their worth

at night I lay with them
when sleep wouldn't come
after midnight
and before four

my AMs
of the soul
as wakefulness
became my friend

and so did Leonard Cohen
as I knew he would

*Proem: "She walked barefoot on hard rocks. They only see her teetering not daring." — Author*

# Emily Dickinson

sometimes
after studious seclusion
she spoke
her conversation classically cultivated
not to boast
complained too often people said, "What?"
so gave up trying to talk
and thus sent notes

and wrote and wrote and wrote
poems
created with log-cabin efficiency
level lines hewn longhand
solid roof shape
safe from bear or beast
wandering deer curious
yet shy coming upon symmetry

raccoon return
for back-door give-away feast
embers of humanity
emanating from hearth
and her home, surrounded by wild-flower dignity
tangled vines
dark underbrush
all rooted in good black earth

life thoughts simplicity
death thoughts morbidity
long hours of lingering mystery
accepting that they are

will be there
for eternity

## Song of Whitman and the Black Man

You may have read
Walt Whitman's poem all the way through
songs about himself.
You may often go back and re-read
the part where he comes upon a Negro man,
a runaway,
sitting on his woodpile.

Your heart breezes balmy
as he assures him
and leads him
all limpsy into the house,
loosens
as he fills a tub to wash away sweat and awkwardness,
warms
as he slaves to heal his bruised feet
and the galls of his neck and ankles,
warms further through
as he clothes him
and welcomes him to sit at the table.

Your heart glows
at his recuperation
then accepts it is his time to pass on north.
You may be determined to master this noble manner,
hope you have the courage,
remembering that this whole week,
the gun
fire-locked
leaned in the corner,

the only prisoner
held captive by kindness.

## promise of rainbow

at what age is it
that
you find out
that

your mom telling you about the rainbow's end
keeps your mind on treasures to come
and not the storm that's just passed

or no matter how big they seem
Daddy Long-Legs do not bite

or one summer day
when your head pops out of the lake
it signals the brain
that
your arms and legs have grown long enough
to tread water

when
is not important

at what time in your life do you find out
that sitting down across the table with foes
breaking bread
fear and anger freeze-dries and shatters to the floor

spring's changing light
tells you about the earth's shift in axis
informing the soil it is soft enough for rebirth

your poetry becomes not simply bare thoughts
from one raw soul to one more
but veritably warm honey
lining the inner core of another

when
is not important

# Hot Glass Poem #1

Don't just look at glass. Dance your eyes over the sparkling pieces.
Peer deeply into the dimensions.
Take a breath and float your eyes over the surface.

Working with glass is an emotional experience
you will come to understand
when you think of it as a creation in a molten state.
It is the most fluid three-dimensional medium
an artist can work closely with.

The sensual flow holds you in a magic spell.
The glass is only cold, hard, brittle and fragile
when it comes back down to room temperature.
For the artist the process is a hot ballet of whirling and twirling,
blowing and twisting, drooping and swinging the glass.

Imagine glass made viscous from intense heat
with the flames licking the sides of its shape
transforming it towards timeless suspension.

At a precise spontaneous moment, he or she decides to stop
and freeze it in time by taking it out of the fire,
where it becomes quickly rigid.

Now you can appreciate the art of glass.

## Hot Glass Poem #2

My energy is here not created or destroyed
I am matter
I am matter
and I am joy.

Walk your eyes to the fire, to access the door
get closer, glowing closer to the furnace roar.

Let loose, melt the tension wiggle, wiggle.
Let emotion run, run and sizzle.

Wine and conversation over all the din,
Clink your glass, 'cause your brain won't win.

Shears, jacks, paddles, blocks and newspaper galore.
Listen for the soft-shoe-shuffle on the dance floor.

Squeeze me; squeeze me glass into a sphere.
But don't take too long perfection; could take years.

Yellow flames lick the sides of my sensuous shape.
Cold tools against my hot skin thin my nape.

Dodge my hot ballet, orange wave swinging in the room.
Then back to the red heat, zoom, zoom, zoom, zoom.

Art, civility scares us, so arguing is kept at bay
See what goes. Laughing and teasing have their way.

Steady breaths from your centre root into the void,
purest creation into wire atmosphere, searing asteroid.

Art explores your shadows; ignore all your burns.
Feast your eyes. I'm basking in glory. It's my turn.

Transform sensual flow frozen in magic pureness.
Sparkling hunger quickens the soul for private stillness.

# ACKNOWLEGMENTS

**Roommates**
*Published Canadian Woman Studies*
*Vol 33, No 1-2 (2018-2019): Women's Human Rights*

**Gotta Have It Once a Month Green Dream Jelly Bean**
*(spoken poetry night 2012 Chancery Art Gallery, ON)*

**White Silence**
*Published in Canadian Woman Studies Magazine Vol 22 No. 2 (2003) Women and Peace-Building*

**Sarajevo**
*Published Descant Magazine Spring (2012)*

**Listen to You**
*Published poetry night Anthology, Muskoka Nov. (2005)*

**Beautiful Black**
*Published in Canadian Woman Studies Magazine Vol 36 No. 1, 2 (2023) The Black and Indigenous Leadership Issue*

**When I Am, Me**
*Published in Canadian Woman Studies Magazine Vol 36 No. 1, 2 (2023) The Black and Indigenous Leadership Issue*

**A Breast of a World**
*Published poetry night Anthology, Muskoka Nov. (2005)*

**For the Second Time**
*Published in Canadian Woman Studies Magazine Vol 21, No 3 (2002) Women and Sport*

**Emily Dickinson**
*Published in Canadian Woman Studies Magazine Vol 36 No. 1, 2 (2023) The Black and Indigenous Leadership Issue*

**Song of Whitman and the Black Man**
*Published in Canadian Woman Studies Magazine Vol 36 No. 1, 2 (2023) The Black and Indigenous Leadership Issue*

**Hot Glass Poem #1**
*Broadcast CBC Radio One — Outfront (2001)*

**Hot Glass Poem #2**
*Broadcast CBC Radio One — Outfront (2001)*

## AUTHOR PROFILE

Kathy Ashby was born in Thunder Bay, Ontario CANADA. She is an artist, writer and a member of the League of Canadian Poets. Her writing has appeared in: Toronto Star, Muskoka Magazine, National Glass Gazette, Ontario Craft Council Magazine, Artichoke Magazine, Rable.ca and Chicken Soup for the Soul.

Kathy studied art and design at Sheridan College, Mississauga, Ontario, 1972-74 and majored in Glassblowing in her final year. She first publicly demonstrated the art of blowing glass at Harbourfront Craft Studios' inaugural year of 1974.

In 2004 Kathy was nominated for a YWCA, Woman of Distinction Award, in the Arts Category.In 2009, Kathy received an Ontario Arts Council Grant to complete her first fiction manuscript.

Kathy lives with her husband, Brian, in rural Muskoka, Ontario, Canada.

www.ingramcontent.com/pod-product-compliance
Lightning Source LLC
Chambersburg PA
CBHW071722020426
42333CB00017B/2361